The Holy
ROSARY
of Mary, The Beloved

A Devotional to Mary Magdalene

"To the Lady Chosen by God, and to her children, she whom I love in the truth--and not I only, but also all who know the truth--because of the truth which lives in us and will be with us forever..."

2 *John* 1 & 2

THE HOLY
ROSARY
OF MARY, THE BELOVED

A Devotional to Mary Magdalene

CONTENTS

Acknowledgments

The drawings in this devotional were done by Roe Halper for her book *Tears of the Prophets,* Bayberry Press, Westport, Connecticut, 1975, introduction by Rabbi Alexander M. Schindler, President, Union of American Hebrew Congregations, and are used with the permission of the artist.

The drawing of Barbara Harris was done by Jacques Schickel of Brookfield, Vermont.

The quotation from the *Cloud of Unknowing* is from Image Books, edited by William Johnston, S.J., Doubleday, New York, 1973, and is used with the permission of the publisher.

A direct quotation is taken from the King James Version of the Bible. Other translations that have been used for reference are: the Revised Standard Version; the New International Version; the Good News Bible; the New English Bible with Apocrypha (Oxford Study Edition); the Jerusalem Bible; and the New Jerusalem Bible.

Translations of the Bible are referred to in light of today's scholarly consensus advising reliance not on any one English translation, but use of the several available translations in an intelligent and creative way (see, *e.g.,* Daniel J. Harrington, S.J., *Interpreting the New Testament--A Practical Guide,* Michael Glazier, Inc., Wilmington, Delaware, 1979; reprinted The Liturgical Press (Order of St. Benedict, Inc.), Collegeville, Minnesota, 1990, 149pp., p. 40).

Typesetting for this book has been done by Computer Access & Training, Montpelier, Vermont.

First publication July 22, 1990, by Sophia Press, Montpelier, Vermont. Copyright 1991 by Lloyd K. Moyer. All rights reserved.

International Standard Book Number 0-9631507-0-7.

Library of Congress Catalog Card Number: 92-80734.

FOREWORD

"This book will make a traveller of thee,
If by its counsel thou wilt ruled be;
It will direct thee to the Holy Land,
If thou wilt its directions understand..."

John Bunyan, *The Pilgrim's Progress,*
from the Author's Apology for his Book

DEDICATION

"Women of Jerusalem, I am dark and beautiful..."

Song of Songs, 1:5

For the RT. REV. BARBARA C. HARRIS,

on the occasion of her presence for the consecration of an icon to Mary Magdalene, Grace Cathedral, San Francisco, July 22, 1990.

THE RIGHT REVEREND BARBARA C. HARRIS,

BISHOP OF THE CHURCH OF GOD

Suffragan Bishop,
The Episcopal Diocese of Massachusetts

INTRODUCTION

"Sweet was the love between Mary and Jesus. How she loved him! How much more he loved her! Do not take the Gospel account lightly, as if it were some superficial tale. It depicts their relationship in utter truth. Reading it, who could fail to see that she loved him intensely, withholding nothing of her love, and refusing the comfort of anything less than his love in return...", writes the anonymous English author of the 14th century *Cloud of Unknowing*, at the beginning of Chapter 22, on the relationship of Jesus with Mary Magdalene.

What of this woman, a contemporary of Jesus, who appears with him at the very start of his public ministry; who accompanied him throughout his ministry; who was there at his crucifixion, death and burial; and who was the one to whom he returned first, to whom he spoke, and with whom he spent time first following his resurrection? Mary Magdalene is the only woman, and in truth the only person man or woman, mentioned in scripture at all these critical stages of Jesus' adult life. She was chosen by him to be his "apostle to the apostles", bringing the news of his resurrection to the apostles. Mystics, poets, and scholars agree that she was the leading woman in the group accompanying him.

Mysteriously and intriguingly the most well-known traditions say she later went to Ephesus, the residence of the woman addressed by John in his Second Letter: *Eklekte Kyria*-- the Chosen Lady--a lady, apparently a widow with a grown family (consisting of both natural and spiritual children?), who John assures us was well-acquainted "from the beginning" with Jesus, a Jesus who John is at great pains in his letter to show was a fully incarnate man as well as God.

May this Rosary devotional give to whom it will eyes to see Mary Magdalene with Jesus, in a way that is true to scripture and to the tradition, on her feast day of July 22, 1990, at the consecration of an icon to her in Grace Cathedral, San Francisco, and in time to come.

FIRST JOYFUL MYSTERY

The Birth and Youth of the Lord (*Luke* 1:26 - 2)

The Lady's Message: Mary, the mother of my Beloved, heard with joy the message that she had been chosen to bring God's son into the world. Yet, as she was only a young girl, she was troubled, and went to visit her older cousin, Elizabeth. When she heard that Elizabeth, even as an old woman, was also pregnant, with a child who would be God's messenger for her son, her spirit was reassured. She accepted her role in God's plan, and praised the name of God.

Her joy became complete when the baby was born. She remembered God's words to her, even though the birth took place in the straw of a stable manger. Her loving nurture and the firm kindness of Joseph raised Jesus as a young boy of Israel, following all the requirements of the law.

But, even upon Jesus' entrance into early manhood during the Passover celebration, he left his family and remained behind in the Temple, to question and listen to the teachers of the law there. Mary and Joseph noticed him missing, and in great anxiety returned to find him.

She then began to understand that her son's world would reach far beyond that of her motherhood and her family. We honor her for accepting as well this part of God's plan which continued to cause her such pain, giving us a complete example of motherhood.

Prayer: Dear Blessed Lady, together with You, we honor Mary, the mother of your Beloved, God's son. May the example of her devotion as a mother in the early years, and her later courage through her sorrow in seeing who her son was and beginning to let him go, be honored by all who love and honor Jesus. *Amen.*

"The Lord possessed me in the beginning of his Way, before his works of old...

then, I was by him as one brought up with him, and I was daily his delight, rejoicing always before him..."

Proverbs 8:22 *et seq.*

from Fourth Joyful Mystery,

The Marriage of the Lady

SECOND JOYFUL MYSTERY

The Birth and Youth of the Lady ("I was made in eternity, from the beginning, before the world began...", *Proverbs* 8:23)

The Lady's Message: God's plan involved me, and through me all women and men. I was my Beloved's hidden treasure and pearl of great price. Through love, all that he had and all that he was were mine.

The angels announced my birth to my mother Anna. She and my father Joachim treasured this in their hearts. I was fortunate among the young girls of Israel to have been taught the Torah. Later, due to my father's devotion, and his prominence in the synagogue, I went to Jerusalem, where I studied with the doctors of the law.

I was scorned and laughed at by many, who thought it was not fitting for a daughter of Israel to seek place in the councils of men. Yet, my spirit was strong, and the devoted support of my mother and father always maintained me.

When I returned home with my parents, my spirit became free, and my family was troubled. God's law was still in my heart, but I was seeking liberation from the painful rejection I had known among the scribes, pharisees and doctors of law in Jerusalem.

Love, and not the respectability sought by my parents as a daughter of Israel, was to be the solution to my pain.

Just as love, and not kingship or grandeur, was the purpose of my Beloved.

Prayer: Dear Blessed Lady, we see in your rejection by the doctors of the law, the rejection of the possibilities of all women by false religion and authority through the ages. Through your spirit, the daughters of Israel, and all women, gain vindication and take their full place in human society, as is God's plan. May the scorn you suffered and the example of your courage show God's will to all women and men, in every age. *Amen.*

"He gave me the courage to let go of the fury of my past doubtings
and seeking, to lose them in the oneness that he offered with himself."

from Fourth Joyful Mystery, *The Marriage of the Lady*

THIRD JOYFUL MYSTERY

The Young Womanhood of the Lady ("Then Myriam...took a tambourine in her hand, and all the women followed her with tambourines and dancing." *Exodus* 15:20)

The Lady's Message: The Galilee of my youth was a crossroads for all cultures--Greeks, Romans, Jews and the ancient cultures of our ancestors. I did not want to miss any of it. My parents were dismayed as I, a young woman, would engage on my own men and women from everywhere in spirited conversation. And I would dance before admiring men and women.

I did not wish to hurt my parents, and I esteemed the great women of Israel; but my spirit was too strong simply to be given in marriage. My calling from God drove me to learn about all people, and to express my beauty in song and dancing as well. And so, I learned all that could be known about the minds, hearts and passions of men and women.

I did as my Beloved did, pulling all people into me and making them all a part of me. For this I as a woman was scorned as shameless. But I did not listen. I risked the rejection of the elders and my family, for I knew I was doing it out of passion for the God of Israel, and that this was what God wanted me to be doing.

God, my heavenly Mother, and the Mother of all Israel's great women through the ages.

Prayer: Dear Blessed Lady, you ignored the ridicule you received as a young woman, and fearlessly gained knowledge of all conditions of life. In this you were drawing women everywhere to follow your example, and gaining the respect of men as their peer. Through your spirit, teach us that this is the will of God, for women as for men. *Amen.*

"Your lips cover me with kisses; your love is better than wine;
there is a fragrance about you...no wonder all women love you...

How beautiful you are my love...how perfect you are!...

Come with me from Galilee, my Bride; come with me from Lebanon!"

Song of Songs, passim

FOURTH JOYFUL MYSTERY

The Marriage of the Lady ("The Lord possessed me in the beginning of his Way, before his works of old...then, I was by him as one brought up with him, and I was daily his delight...", *Proverbs* 8:22-31;   *Psalm* 45:10-17; *Isaiah* 54)

The Lady's Message: I was of the House of David. I had known and seen Jesus, as our towns were not far apart, and we were distant kin. Though I respected my lineage, I had avoided ancestral gatherings, desiring to be free. Both my Beloved and I had lived a youth of freedom, following our own individual callings from God. This caused pain and concern to each of us individually and to our families and town elders. Then, we both attended one assembling of David's House, on the shores of the Lake of Galilee.

We met, and we did not think of our families at that moment of meeting, only of each other. His kindness, and yet the force and compelling intensity of his presence, gave me the courage to let go of the fury of my past doubtings and seeking, to lose them in the oneness that he offered with himself.

He had felt the calling to be free from all ties of family to do God's will. He needed me to help him gain that freedom, through my love. I could see that my calling had been the same, and my need for him was the same.

"Your lips cover me with kisses; your love is better than wine.
There is a fragrance about you;...no wonder all women love you...

How beautiful you are my love! How your eyes shine with love behind your veil.
Your breasts are like gazelles, twin deer feeding among the lilies...
How beautiful you are my love; how perfect you are!...

Our love is powerful as death; our passion strong as death itself.
It bursts into flame, and burns like a raging fire...

My lover is one in ten thousand...he is mine, and I am his;...

If a man offered all the wealth of his house for love, he would be utterly scorned...
Let the king have young women without number...I love only one;...

Come with me from Galilee, my Bride; come with me from Lebanon!"

Prayer: Dear Blessed Lady, you gave up your individual freedom not in response to the desires of your parents, nor from the promptings of society, but as an act of your own will, done out of love. You fulfilled every letter of the law, not by conforming to the letter, but by love. Give the grace of your spirit to all women similarly to remain faithful to themselves, granting to those you will the happiness you found, as a choice of love. *Amen.*

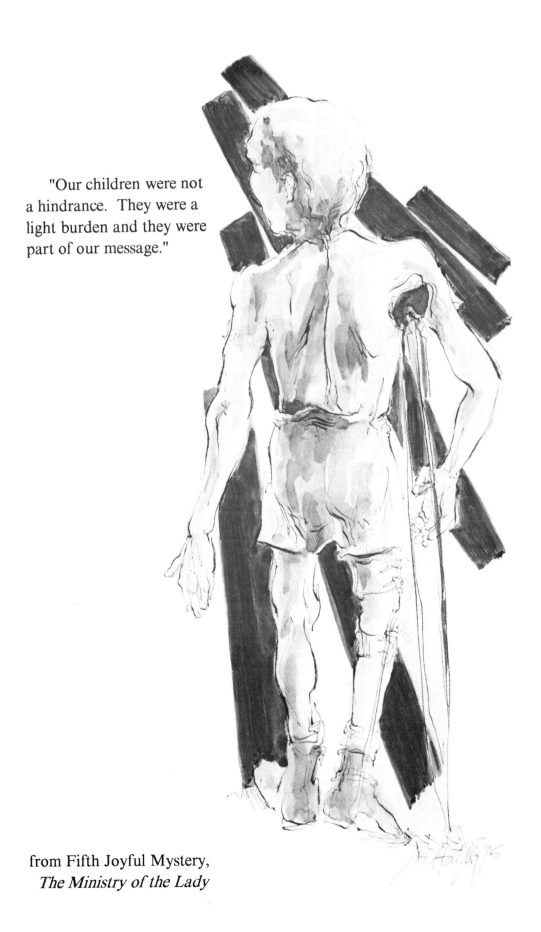

"Our children were not
a hindrance. They were a
light burden and they were
part of our message."

from Fifth Joyful Mystery,
The Ministry of the Lady

FIFTH JOYFUL MYSTERY

The Ministry of the Lady (*Luke* 8; *Mark* 3:20-35; 15:30-47; *Matthew* 28)
("...He listened to me, waiting daily at my doorway...He heeded my instruction
he did not refuse it...and, he became wise...", from *Proverbs* 8:33-4;
"From the beginning, his only command to me was that I walk in love...",
from 2 *John* 5,6)

The Lady's Message: We had become one, as the God of Israel is One, and intends men and women to become One--out of love. Love was our message, and our only message. But, as a disciplined love, it became a message of great power, overcoming every evil in the world. We had no home, but went from village to village in Galilee and Judea, attracting men and women to follow us.

We had children together, as did other men and women who came with us; yet all children were our children. Our children were not a hindrance--they were a light burden and they were part of our message--though at times some in our group had to be reminded of this.

I was the leader of the group of women: Joanna, Susannah, Salome and many others. My Beloved brought Peter, James, John and others in to form the men's group of disciples. His power as a man was compelling, but even greater was his kindness to all men and women in need.

He taught that to form our new society--the kingdom on earth reflecting the kingdom of heaven-- former family ties, marriages, children and possessions may have to be left behind altogether, without hesitation.

Joanna left her husband and her high place in Herod's court, risking danger to be with us.

Peter in obedience to him left behind his wife, children and everything he owned to stay with our group.

Jesus himself followed the way he had proclaimed, allowing his father and mother, and sisters and brothers, to stay with us when they would only on the basis of doing God's will, and not out of any blood ties or family relationship.

Prayer: Dear Blessed Lady, help women and men alike to follow your example, and not be afraid to put even our most intimate ties and our most valuable possessions in a secondary place to God's kingdom. Make human for us the often hard and sharp-edged teachings of Jesus, that things most dear to us may have to be taken out of our lives and left behind, for our own sake and for love. Help us to remember as well his joyful teaching, that whatever is then possessed in love will never have to be left behind. *Amen.*

"His power as a man was compelling, but even greater was his kindness to all men and women in need..."

from Fifth Joyful Mystery,
The Ministry of the Lady

First Sorrowful Mystery

The Agony in the Garden   (*Luke* 22:39-44)

The Lady's Message: Many of the women in the group had wanted Jesus to establish a kingdom by force, to protect his wonderful works of love by force of arms. They supported Peter and others in their desire to fight for his freedom. I did not want to lose him, but I knew this was not his Way.

After we women had helped serve the final Passover meal, we withdrew with the children and left the men with Jesus. Though he had offered bread and wine as his own body and blood at the meal, the men still had not learned, and were continuing to dispute among themselves about who would hold first place in God's kingdom. I knew how this pained Jesus.

The women were little better, seeking preference in the Kingdom for their sons, forgetting the sacrifice he was making, and clamoring for protection from the threat of official action. I calmed their fears.

As Jesus prayed, I wept while he agonized and sweat in prayer, fearful of the time that our true protection would be taken away from us.

Prayer: Dear Blessed Lady, you opened yourself up to God for help, and did not seek protection in earthly power or seek to have your Beloved establish a kingdom by force on earth. Give your grace to other women and men, that in the times of agony in their lives they might not seek to build false walls of security, but continue to be open to the will of God, even when the result might seem bitter. *Amen.*

23

"Many of the women in the
group had wanted Jesus to
establish a kingdom
by force..."

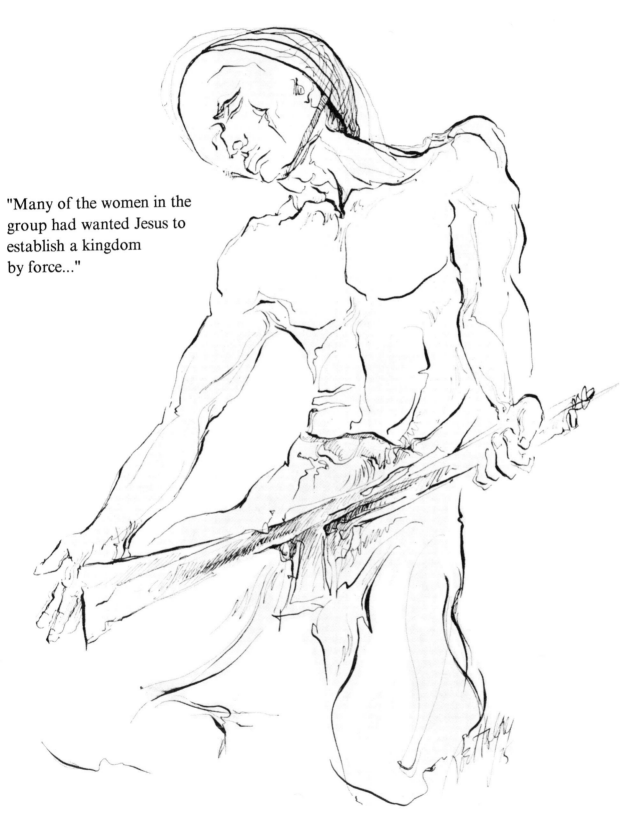

from First Sorrowful Mystery,
The Agony in the Garden

24

"...I knew that force was not his Way..."

SECOND SORROWFUL MYSTERY

The Scourging   (*Mark* 15:1-15)

The Lady's Message: Peter had denied that he ever knew Jesus, and the men had run away and gone into hiding. I and the women stayed. We were not in danger. We were seen as no threat by the authorities.

As the soldiers began to whip Jesus, the rage of my defiance rose within me, though I said nothing. I felt the whip tearing his flesh as though they were whipping me. I joined my soul with his to ease the pain, and glared at the Romans as an act of resistance.

The power of the state could crush the body, but it could not break the bond of our fidelity-- the fidelity of God.

Prayer: Dear Blessed Lady, in your faithfulness you were beaten with the same scourging Jesus received, and you felt the pain no less. Teach us by your endurance that the example of a woman's fidelity can give strength to both women and men in the face of tyranny and injustice. *Amen.*

"The kingdom of love that we all had known together...the power overcoming every illness, evil and death, received its most bitter mockery as the soldiers put a crown of thorns on his head and spit on him."

from Third Sorrowful Mystery,
The Crowning with Thorns

27

THIRD SORROWFUL MYSTERY

The Crowning with Thorns (*Matthew* 27:27-31)

The Lady's Message: The kingdom of love that he, I, the children, and all the men and women who came with us had known together, the power that all had seen overcoming every illness, evil and death, received its most bitter mockery as the soldiers put a crown of thorns on his head and spit on him.

I said nothing, as he said nothing, not out of contempt, much less defeat. We said nothing more in memory of all that we had done, and in the knowledge that the same power could have ended the present cruelty, if it had chosen to do so.

The power to have stopped the madness that was occurring was not used, simply to allow it to take place. The harshness of the soldiers was caused by their rage at being faced with goodness, a goodness they could not understand and therefore wanted to destroy. Their harshness was allowed in order to give an example to humanity of every age.

Prayer: Dear Blessed Lady, your love was tested in this mockery of the kingdom you had known on earth. Help us to overcome our own bitterness and sense of defeat, as you overcame them, knowing that the cruelest mockery can crush the body but cannot crush the spirit. *Amen.*

"Looking at me, he comforted our own children, and the other women and their children as well..."

from Fourth Sorrowful Mystery, *The Carrying of the Cross*

"His tone was edged with bitterness..."

FOURTH SORROWFUL MYSTERY

The Carrying of the Cross (*Mark* 15:20-25; *Luke* 23:26-31)

The Lady's Message: I, the women from Galilee and Jerusalem, and our children, walked together, as a stranger, Simon of Cyrene, helped Jesus carry his cross to the hill of skulls, the place of execution.

My spirit was resolute, and I did not weep, though the others did. Looking at me, he comforted our own children, and the other women and their children as well. His tone was edged with bitterness.

The cross is the symbol of the state's power to put to death those who are a threat to it. The state, in whatever form it takes, will do this because it wants to be seen as the final authority in the affairs of men and women.

But a dimension beyond any form of the state is the true final authority, and this truth cannot be touched even by the ultimate actions of torture and execution.

Prayer: Dear Blessed Lady, you were not afraid to walk to the place set aside by the state for public execution. As the chosen daughter of Israel, God's Daughter, teach us by your example to show the same courage and resolute spirit, having your faith that no form of persecution or death can overcome the power of God within us. *Amen.*

"Worldly authorities, jealous of
his power, cruelly killed him..."

"...I wept bitterly, and only my spirit of defiance at the cruelties that had taken place kept me from dying as well."

from Fifth Sorrowful Mystery,
The Crucifixion

FIFTH SORROWFUL MYSTERY

The Crucifixion (*Matthew* 27:55-61; *Mark* 15:40-47; *Luke* 23:47-56; *John* 19:25-42)

The Lady's Message: We were all there: I, Joanna, Salome, Mary (Cleopas' wife), and all the women who had been with us from the start. I and Jesus' mother walked to the foot of the cross as my Beloved was dying.

He gave his mother into the care of our dear friend John, as John would be watchful of myself and our children as well. I heard him cry that God had forsaken him, and then he died.

This time I wept bitterly, and only my spirit of defiance at the cruelties that had taken place kept me from dying as well.

I rejoined the group of women, and we returned to the house in Jerusalem where we had been staying. Later, we joined Joseph of Arimathea to wrap Jesus' body in linen and place it in the tomb.

Prayer: Dear Blessed Lady, your spirit was not crushed, nor was your love destroyed, even on the death of your Beloved. Give us the courage you showed as a woman, to know our grief but still to take action for those we love, even in their suffering and death. *Amen.*

"I rejoined the group of women...later we joined Joseph of Arimathea to wrap Jesus' body in linen and place it in the tomb."

from Fifth Sorrowful Mystery,
The Crucifixion

FIRST GLORIOUS MYSTERY

The Resurrection   (*Matthew* 28:1-10; *Mark* 16:1-14; *Luke* 24:1-11; *John* 20:1-18)

The Lady's Message: I was in deep sorrow and grief during the following day Sabbath, and the other women comforted me. We had spent some time calming our children and seeing to their comfort as well. Peter and the men had been in contact with us and their presence strengthened us. I left everyone as soon as the Sabbath was over, and went to the tomb while it was still dark.

The tomb was empty! I ran back to tell Peter and John.

They looked and left, but I could not leave.

I wept bitterly, alone at the tomb. Then I heard a voice, and heard my name spoken!

Jesus stood there...he kissed me...he was alive!

We sat and talked for hours, recalling all that together we had seen and done. Then he told me that he was to be taken to heaven, but would come back again in a human body to reassure the men, in Galilee. We kissed again. Then his body vanished.

I ran back to tell the men! At first they would not believe me, but then they went ahead into Galilee.

Prayer: Dear Blessed Lady, Jesus returned alive to you before all others to let you know that the love between himself and you was not dead, but lived on. You were one with him, the mother to his children, his apostle to the apostles, chosen first as his Beloved to see him and to know that he had overcome death. As you helped overcome the doubts of the men, may you also help to overcome our doubts, and give us faith that love does not die. *Amen.*

"...He kissed me! He was alive!"

from First Glorious Mystery,
The Resurrection

SECOND GLORIOUS MYSTERY

The Ascension   (*Acts:* 1:1-14)

The Lady's Message: Jesus returned to me and our children many times during the following 40 days. He asked me to bring together the group of women and the other children and he spoke with us.

The women were to go back into their lives, bringing as many of their family and friends into the group as they could. I was the one he spoke directly to first, as I had always been.

I and the women joined the men, his mother and the members of his own family in prayer, nearly every day.

I was not surprised when he was taken into heaven, as he had told me of this, and he had left our private meetings before in the same way.

Prayer: Dear Blessed Lady, nothing that Jesus did was done without your knowledge. He wanted to show you, and through you all ages, that the love he had known with you forms the basis of true living between men and women, on earth as in heaven. Teach us through your example, and the example of the women you sent out to do God's will, that relationships between men and women, formed in love, desire and faith, are the cornerstone of true society, on earth and through eternity. *Amen.*

"During the following 40 days...he asked me to bring
together the group of women and the other children...
and he spoke to us."

from Second Glorious Mystery,
The Ascension

THIRD GLORIOUS MYSTERY

The Coming of the Holy Spirit   (*Acts* 2:1-41;
                    "To the Lady Chosen by God, and to her children,
                    she whom I love in the truth--and not I only, but
                    also all who know the truth--because of the truth
                    which lives in us and will be with us forever..."
                    2 *John* 1&2)

The Lady's Message: I needed no special reassurance on the Day of Pentecost. I had already spent much time in private with my Beloved.

But, Peter in particular always had a special need for reassurance, and so did many of the other men and women assembled in that room on that great day. I could look on with a quiet joy, as tongues of fire came down, filling everyone with love, and giving everyone power to speak deliriously in all languages.

I smiled and was proud at Peter's energy, greeting everyone and baptizing as many as he could into the fellowship.

Prayer: Dear Blessed Lady, may you help us to bring the fire of your Beloved into our lives, so that we may be remade in the image of God--an image he said was to be found in little children. *Amen.*

"I smiled and was proud at Peter's energy,
greeting everyone and baptizing as many as
he could into the fellowship."

from Third Glorious Mystery,
The Coming of the Holy Spirit

42

FOURTH GLORIOUS MYSTERY

The Assumption of the Lady   (*Psalm* 45:10-17; *Judith* 13:17-20)

The Lady's Message: Jesus taught that in the resurrection men and women do not marry and are not given in marriage. By this he meant that they choose relationship by love, as angels or spiritual beings, and are not given to advance any personal, family or societal purpose as on earth. They freely give themselves to one another, in faithfulness, love, desire and truth.

This can also take place on earth as it does in heaven, and he meant it to be so. He also taught that men and women are to become like children to find this love, and that children, and all who without deceit or guile can be wise as serpents yet still innocent as doves, are like those who live in the kingdom of heaven.

He lived life on earth blamelessly, a second Adam to redeem Adam's sins. In love, I lived blamelessly as well, a second Eve to be with him during his life on earth, and to redeem the sins of Eve.

All who follow us in love will also live blamelessly.

On my death, I was raised body and soul to be with him forever. The same future awaits all men and women who have lived in love on earth.

Prayer: Dear Blessed Lady, through your birth, your steadfast love and your work on earth, you were shown as the second Eve. Your example with that of your Beloved can redeem men and women who follow you in love. Give us the love and desire to be with you and your Beloved both here on earth, and in the life to come. *Amen.*

"...that we may be remade
in the image of God; an image
he said was to be found in little
children."

from Third Glorious Mystery,
The Coming of the Holy Spirit

FIFTH GLORIOUS MYSTERY

The Coronation of the Lady ("Whoever finds me finds life and receives favor from the Lord; whoever fails to find me harms himself; all who hate me love death..." *Proverbs* 8:35-36; *Revelation* 12; 19:7-8; 21:1-4; 22:17; "We are One", from *Genesis* 1:27, 2:24)

The Lady's Message: Scripture tells us that the image of God, when made flesh on earth is man and woman: male and female, one human creation, forming together the image of God. From birth the two are separate, but when they leave father and mother to seek each other, in love they become a new being, one flesh.

So it was with myself and my Beloved. On earth, though he lived in simplicity, he was a king. I was with him as his queen. Worldly authorities, jealous of his power, cruelly killed him. But, he overcame death and with great might came to life again, to live forever.

I live with him in heaven as I lived with him in love on earth.

Prayer: Dear Blessed Lady, may this Holy Rosary deepen the faith and strengthen the hope of all men and women of love, holy desire and good will, that they may live as you lived on earth, and may be with you in the world to come, where you reign as Queen beside the Immortal King of Ages, together One God, now and forever. *Amen.*

"...the image of God, when made flesh on earth,
is man and woman: male and female, one human creation,
forming together the image of God." from *Genesis* 1:27, 2:24

from Fifth Glorious Mystery,
The Coronation of the Lady

HAIL HOLY QUEEN

Hail Holy Queen, Lady of Mercy, Hail our life, our strength and our hope! Poor, banished children of Eve, we cry out to you; we send you our sighs, mourning and weeping in this vale of tears. Turn your eyes of mercy towards us, most gracious advocate; and both in this life and in the life to come, show us the Blessed One, your Beloved, Jesus.

Oh Lady of wisdom, power and might.

Pray for us, Holy Lady of God.

That we may be made worthy of the promises of Christ.

"I was made in eternity, from the beginning, before the world began...whoever finds me finds life, and receives favor from the Lord; whoever fails to find me harms himself; all who hate me love death..."

Proverbs 8:22-3, 35-6

"WE ARE ONE"
from *Genesis* 1:27, 2:24

THE ROSARY PRAYER

Oh God, your only begotten son, by his life, death and resurrection, has purchased for us the rewards of eternal life; grant, we pray, that meditating upon these mysteries of the most Holy Rosary of the Blessed Lady Mary, your daughter, the Beloved of our Lord, we may learn to imitate what they contain and obtain what they promise through the same Christ our Lord.

"The Rosary...is a form of union with God, and has a most uplifting effect on the soul."

Pope John XXIII, commenting on the traditional
rosary in the context of Vatican II.

AFTERWORD

*"What Christian left locked up and went his way,
Sweet Christiana opens with her key..."*

John Bunyan, *The Pilgrim's Progress,*
from the Introduction to the Second Part

About the author:

Lloyd K. Moyer graduated from Harvard and the Faculty of Law at Stockholm University and practiced law for 14 years. He is currently an aspirant for holy orders as a priest in the Episcopal Diocese of Vermont, and lives in Montpelier, Vermont.

The author wishes to acknowledge the people of Christ Church, Montpelier, Vermont, and many other people within and outside the church, for the sharing of our lives, from which this book has come.

DATE DUE

DEC 31			